When the Fairytale Ends

The Journey to Overcome Abuse

Marisa Russo

ISBN 978-1-0980-0501-6 (paperback)
ISBN 978-1-0980-0502-3 (digital)

Christian Faith Publishing, Inc.
832 Park Avenue
Meadville, PA 16335
www.christianfaithpublishing.com

Printed in the United States of America

*My long journey to heal and rebuild
from mental and verbal abuse.*

A detailed memoir through the years.

In loving memory of my loyal companions,
Bubba, Russell, Mickey, Lily and Toby.

Foreword

They say that the "eyes are the windows to your soul." When people look at me, what do they see? Do they see the shattered dreams? Do they see the flashbacks that constantly play in my mind? Do they see the sadness within me? Through my smile, can they see the scars that my soul carries?

My purpose in writing this personal memoir is to educate others about emotional and verbal abuse and help another person—help them realize that it's not their fault, they are not crazy, and it is the abuser who is brainwashing them to believe their lies. There have been some people who have made me feel guilty about the abuse, saying that if I had been strong enough, it never would have happened. That is not true. Abuse can happen to anyone. Never in my wildest dreams did I imagine that I would end up in an abusive marriage. No one knows the amount of pain that I felt in my heart nor did they see the destruction of his wrath when I tried to stand up to him. I was so lost, and I was scared. I had put my hopes and dreams into his hands, but ultimately, he destroyed them and robbed me of so many years of my life. The fairytale I had once dreamed of since I was a little girl was now over. I thought I had my fairytale, but I ended up in a nightmare, one which I was not able to wake up from.

People have often said to me in the past (even currently), "Why didn't you just leave?" "Why didn't you just kick him out?" "Why did you allow him to do that to you?" "Why didn't you see the red flags?" "Did you really think he was going to change?" In addition to the above statements, post-abuse, I have heard, "Oh, there are worse things that could have happened to you" or "there is always someone worse off than you." My first reaction was to tell them off. How could they say that? Do they not realize how much emotional pain and suffering I had endured? There was no escape. I was mentally beaten down, constantly walking on eggshells and always in fear of making a mistake because his wrath was brutal. For me, when people make those remarks, it almost makes me feel "guilty," like everything was my fault and that I deserved this.

I will admit that while watching the movie *What's Love Got to Do with It* back in 1993, I was nineteen years old and had not experienced much of life, and therefore, I would say, "Why did she stay with him?" To me, it looked like it was an easy thing to do—just walk out! In fact, because he did not "beat me," I had not even realized that I was being abused until I was removed from that house, "my torture chamber." To my knowledge, there was only one kind of abuse—physical abuse. It was through therapy I had learned I was emotionally, verbally, and financially abused. I thought I was crazy. When I met with therapists while living in New York, they had diagnosed me as having a bipolar disorder. I would walk in telling them that I felt like I was having a nervous breakdown. Unfortunately, at that time in 2005, some counselors had not been fully trained to pick up on "battered women syndrome."

*****

Throughout my life, I have always felt "different." I just never seemed to "fit in." People rejected me. They never allowed me into their cliques. I was constantly bullied to the point where I wanted to quit school. People hated me. Most of them did not even know me. They were just "following the leader." When I was in the tenth grade, a "friend" of mine told me that she could no longer be friends with me because if people saw her with me, they would hate her too. That hurt me so much. I was so lonely. I wanted to belong, but I knew that was never going to happen. My self-worth was based on people's opinion of me. I wanted to be pretty with a "gorgeous figure" and wear amazing clothes. I wanted to be like all the "popular" girls. I hated myself. I was angry and sad.

When I was fifteen, I had my first drink, vodka. I felt great because it numbed the pain. I thought that by drinking, people would then like me and accept me. I started drinking more often. I had a friend who loved to drink, so I followed. When I entered the tenth grade, my grades started plummeting, my attention span was gone, and when I got home from school, I pushed my homework aside. I thought, *Well, if Natalie doesn't do her homework, why should I?* My personality was even changing. I was having violent outbursts, constantly fighting with my parents and sister. During the fights, I would throw things and even raise my hands to my parents. I was horrible. The anger inside of me was getting stronger and stronger.

Growing up, I was no stranger to fights. My parents were wonderful, loving parents who were always there for their children; however, there were a lot of fights.

Contents

The Fairytale

"Get ready, the storm is coming."

After Brian left me, I sent him an e-mail, begging him to come home. He told me that he was never coming back and that I should "get ready, the storm is coming." He was so cold. He broke my heart in every way possible. I wanted to die. I didn't think I had a future. To me, my life was over because at that time, I thought that Brian was my life.

October 2, 2005

I married Brian, the man who I thought would love me for the rest of my life. My wedding day, all the way from the dress to the church and reception, was a fairytale, the one I always dreamed of having. There was only one problem—the groom standing next to me was not my "prince." He would prove to be what everyone thought he was, evil. People always say, "Trust your gut," and it's true, very true. I had that feeling in my stomach, but I ignored it and here I am, fourteen years later, writing this story.

*****

The summer of 2002 was an amazing summer. I was down the shore every weekend, having the time of my life with my friends. I was twenty-eight and free to do what I wanted to do. This was also the last summer for a very long time that I would experience so much joy. I met Brian in April of 2003 and after that, my life took an unexpected turn of events. I thought I was going to finally have my fairytale ending, but instead, I entered a nightmare, one which I could not wake up from.

Over the course of our marriage and even post separation and post divorce, I was subjected to numerous name-calling. Here are just a few: jingle bells, incompetent, worthless, failure, pig, slob, fat, crazy, monster, loser, stupid, etc. He even told many people that he did not marry me for my brains. He has constantly ridiculed me in front of other people. Brian told me that people thought I was stupid and I am better off just being quiet at gatherings. He scolded me, bossed me around, and talked about me right in front of me as if I did not exist. I felt as if I was everything he spoke over me. I was trying to figure out how to be a perfect wife and person because I wanted him to be happy with me and our life.

One witness was my aunt. We were driving to lunch and it was me, my dad, Brian, and Aunt Lucy. Brian was sitting in the front seat with my dad and he was going on about how "he did not marry me for my brains." My aunt was appalled and knew he was abusive.

His anger was always raging. I never knew what I was going to do or say to set him off. I walked on eggshells every day. He would damage walls, cabinets, doors, furniture, and personal property of mine. There were times that he even hurt my animals because he knew how much I loved them, and he enjoyed watching me cry as he hurt them. Since it was "my fault" for his anger, unhappiness, miserable life, and existence, it was "my punishment."

In April 2006, he kicked the cabinet so hard that he hurt his toe to the point where he thought it was broken. As usual, he blamed me for "making" him kick the cabinet. Brian said that if I didn't get him so mad, he wouldn't have to destroy the house. The best part is that all I did was try to stick up for myself during one of his "let me tell you what is wrong with you" sessions. Because "no" was not an option as it would set off his wrath, I had to take him to St. Anthony's Hospital to get his toe checked out. It was broken. Even though I knew deep down it wasn't my fault, I still felt guilty like it *really* was my fault. I truly believed that I was the one ruining the marriage.

There were times that Brian would become so enraged because I was not doing things his way or I wasn't being "perfect" that he would say, "Go in your office right now and get me something of yours that I can break and if you don't get me something, I will go in there myself and break something that I know you really care about." I would go in and get something and he would break it right in front of me, just like he said he would.

Brian constantly blamed me for the problems in the marriage and for everything that went wrong. I was the bad one, the one who destroyed everything. He made sure everyone knew. I walked around with such shame and sadness. This was my world. He would tell me, "Suck it up."

In addition to letting others know I was the problem in the marriage, Brian would also tell everyone that I have a mental illness and that I am crazy and a "pill popper." Before I met Brian, I never saw a mental health ward and I was only on two medications for some depression and anxiety. Since Brian, I have seen three mental health ward facilities and my medications went from being two daily to six daily. Sadly, after a while, I started to think that I was going crazy on top of ruining my marriage. Marisa was gone. The girl I used to be no longer existed. Now there was just pain, in my mind and in my heart.

I had intense crying episodes and horrible depression. Whenever I cried, his torture intensified. He saw a golden opportunity to make himself look like the hero and me the crazy one. People will feel sorry for him because they can now see what he has been dealing with. Brian was worthy of receiving an Academy Award. He knew how to play a victim; he played that part very well. Brian would "push my buttons" until I finally cracked. He would then call 911 and hold the phone up in the air so that the operator could hear me screaming and crying. The cops would then come to the house and a "calm" Brian would suddenly appear, a Dr. Jekyll and Mr. Hyde. He would say to the cops, "My wife is suffering from manic depression and she has psychological issues. I just don't know what to do with her." I just stood there and listened. I was not able to defend myself.

*****

When I first started dating Brian, I met his good friend from high school Andy and his then-fiancé (now wife) Jeanne. Andy would constantly hear about how bad of a wife I was. Andy and Jeanne knew I was being abused, but they also knew that I wouldn't listen to them and I would just end up defending him and blaming myself. When Andy would defend me, Brian would turn around and say, "Well you just don't understand; you don't live with her because if you did, you would end up strangling her. She is that frustrating to live with."

I believe Brian's wish was for me to just die. He would often tell me that the best thing I could do for him was "take my car and drive it off a cliff and kill myself." At times, I wanted to die because I thought that by dying, I would finally find my peace.

Brian would constantly threaten me that he was going to leave me. I heard this daily. In May 2006, he purchased a journal for me. The purpose of this journal was for me to write down all the things I needed to do to make Brian happy and if not, I had to write the consequences. For example, "If I do not make a 360 and change, then Brian will leave me." And if I didn't write in this journal by the time he got home, he said he would leave me. No matter what I did or how hard I tried, it was never good enough—I was never good enough. I really started to believe that I couldn't live without him.

During a fight that he started (which I always got the blame), Brian would say, "That's it, I am leaving you, and I will find someone better than you." And with that, he would walk out of the house. When he did, I ran out and followed him and begged him to come back and to not leave me. I would pull on his shirt or grab his hand to try and pull him back. I was second guessing my sanity, but when I look back now, I wasn't losing my mind, I was losing my self-worth and independence that I once had. If that had been today, I would tell him to just leave and never return, but I had to go through all this pain just to become a much stronger woman.

Whatever happened to him, I always got the blame. If the sky fell, it would be my fault (and he told me this as well). Brian loved motorcycles, but his favorite motorcycle was the "Ducati." He had one previously, but it was totaled after he was hit by a drunk driver some years back. He wanted another one, so in September 2003, after just six months of dating, we went to a dealership to look at some motorcycles for him. I had excellent credit and he did not. I really wanted him to get that bike since I knew how happy it would make him. So I offered to take out a loan for him and he could just give me the money when the bill came in and I would send out the check. It worked out that I did get the loan and he was able to get his Ducati 998. We picked up the motorcycle on his birthday, September 10, 2003. He had made the payments until July 2004 because once I received my settlement, I paid off the balance for him and now he owned it outright. He was very happy, but that happiness didn't last long. Years later he would tell me that by doing what I had done for him had showed him how much I cared for him, but that was (according to Brian) the last time I ever showed him "love."

To him, I was a "monster" who ruined his life. And why? Brian's dream was to make his Ducati into a "super bike" with expense parts that would make it worth over "$100,000." But he never got that dream and therefore, as usual, it was my fault. Brian blamed me for all our financial problems and the reason he couldn't get his dream. Because of this, I was not allowed to spend money on myself. In the meantime, Brian was receiving packages on a weekly basis. It was all motorcycle related (motorcycle parts, jackets, shirts, etc.). I was not allowed to complain because, according to Brian, I already had all my dreams. Brian said, "You have your dream house, had your dream wedding, and you have five dogs, a cat, a bird, and a bunny. What more do you need?" For Brian, it was all about money and material things.

August 2005

Brian used to punch my arm while I was driving if I did something that he thought was stupid. This was the first time he punched my arm while driving. I have always had a fear of driving over bridges. My friend worked with me for a long time to get over this fear. Finally, I was able to drive over the bridge going down the shore with a cigarette and having my friend talk to me very calmly.

By the summer of 2002, I was able to drive over the bridge back and forth alone. Now, Brian and I were on our way to meet our videographer in Belmar to tape the beginning of our wedding video. It had been three years that I had driven over the bridge, and I started to get that fear again. I asked Brian if he would drive, but like usual, he yelled at me and told me it was a stupid fear. I told him that I had to have a cigarette in order to do it, but he would not allow me to have one. He just kept yelling at me, and I became so nervous. As we went over the bridge, I started to hyperventilate, my hands started sweating, and then the feeling that I couldn't swallow came over me so badly that I swerved the car. These were all symptoms that I had in the past, but this was the worst because not only did he yell at me, but he punched my arm. Now I can't even look at a bridge, and as far as driving over one, I would not be able to even if my life depended on it. My fear has even grown to the point where I try to avoid highways as much as I could. I can only drive in the right-hand lane—the lane closest to the shoulder. It gives me a sense of security. If I leave the right-hand lane, I start to get that feeling that I can't swallow and my fear starts to overwhelm me. I still feel like he is sitting in that car yelling at me. I used to always get nervous driving with him because I always got yelled at for something or have my arm punched.

January 2006

Brian made me quit my job because he was not happy with my salary. For Brian, it only meant that he had to pay more than just the mortgage, and he had to contribute to the monthly operating expenses. I was given an ultimatum: get a job in New York City so I can boost my salary or he will stop paying the mortgage and leave me. Brian told me that since I didn't have a degree, this was the only place that I could work and make an additional $20,000 per year. I never liked the city and the thought of working there made me so depressed. But it was either go or lose him, and the thought of losing him was too much to bear.

February 2006

I started my first job in the city. I was now leaving my house at 5:30 a.m. and getting home at 7:45 p.m. I hated the commute and I really hated the "rat race" of New York City. Inside I was hurting, and now I was going to a place every day that I disliked. The life I once had was gone. I felt stuck and so incredibly depressed. The city was so unfamiliar to me.

October 2006

Brian purchased journals for me to write in. He would ask to see the journal when he came home to make sure that I was writing in them because if I didn't, he said he would go to an attorney and leave me. He even had me judge myself on a scale of 1–10. I would consult with him, and he would give me the number. For example, in a couple of entries I would write, "I had my head up my butt today."

November 2006

After being out on disability for six months, I lost my job. They told me that it was due to a merger; therefore, I didn't need to come back. My life was falling apart fast and so was my mind. After losing my job, I started to look for employment back in New Jersey, but he quickly stopped that. I was forced to go back into the city, regardless of how I felt.

Saturday, November 2006

My friend Nicole had purchased me an early birthday gift—tickets to go see *The Grinch Stole Christmas* on Broadway in New York City. That Saturday—the day before the show—we had an argument. As usual, he blamed me for the argument. As a punishment for ruining his day, he told me that I was not allowed to go see the show, and if I did, he would be gone by the time I got home and I would be hearing from his attorney then he would make my life miserable (one of the many repeated threats). I had to call Nicole and tell her that I was not allowed to go. Nicole was extremely upset. I put her on the phone with Brian, and they ended up having an argument. The next day, we went walking around town to all the shops. We went to Irini and I saw a wine glass that I liked. He said that since I was acting normal today, he would buy that glass for me as a reward for being normal.

Sunday, January 7, 2007

My family came over to celebrate my thirty-third birthday. It was my mom, dad, sister, and our friends Jeanne and Andy. While I was cleaning up the dishes in the dining room, I stepped over the baby gate (the gate was put up because the dogs were not allowed in certain parts of the house). Accidentally I tripped over the gate and fell and broke a glass. While I was on the floor, Brian yelled at me for falling and would not even lift a finger to help me out nor did he even ask if I was OK. My dad got angry with him and had some words with him. Everybody was there and saw it for themselves. I could not believe that he could be so cold and not even care about my well-being.

March 2007

I started my next job in March 2007. I was now falling into a much deeper depression. I hated the job and commute, but most of all, I was anxious about Brian not being there at the train station to meet me to go home. That's all I thought about. He would constantly threaten that he was going to leave me, so I was scared he would. I couldn't breathe without him.

Saturday, June 2007

Our friends Mandy and Ethan were having a party at their house in Freehold, New Jersey. Once again, we had an argument which I got blamed for. Brian took his fist and punched the wall in the kitchen and put a huge hole in the wall (photos attached). Then he turned around and said that we are not going to their house, and since I ruined his day, I was not allowed to go to the dog event the next day—the one thing I was looking forward to. It was called *Who Let the Dogs Out* being held by the Warwick Humane Society. He said that if I went, he would be gone by the time I got home and that I would be hearing from his attorney. He also called Mandy and Ethan to tell them that we got into an argument and that we would not be coming. He was very upset that Mandy asked him, "Is Marisa OK?" Brian was sick and tired of women sticking up for other women and how men were always persecuted in the court system.

Later on that night, he gave me a list of outside chores as punishment. He took me around the house to look at the rose bushes and showed me black spots forming on them. He told me that my job was to research this problem and to have an answer to him by that night. Luckily I Googled "black spots on roses" and saw a picture resembling the leaf that I was holding and saw that it was a "fungus." I went to Wadeson's the next day and purchased a spray for them. I was outside for seven hours. My job was to pull weeds, spray the roses, and dig a drench around the plants at the back of the house.

Meanwhile, he went over to Jeanne and Andy's house to watch the motorcycle race with Andy. He called me around 7:00 p.m. and told me that Jeanne and Andy wanted to get ice cream at Bellvalle Farms Creamery and asked me if I wanted to go. I ended up going because I wanted to have a little fun after being stuck outside all day.

August 2007

Brian said that he needed to get a car for himself because having one car is not working anymore. He wanted a pick-up truck. At that time, he still didn't have credit, and my credit was suffering as I had just been discharged from my bankruptcy in March 2007. Unbelievably, he was able to get the loan, but I had to be a cosigner. Once he got the truck, Brian then said his only responsibility was now his truck payment and the mortgage and the rest was going to him and his motorcycle. There was only one problem, he wasn't paying the mortgage. Brian never intended on living there. He had been planning his escape from the day we were married.

September 2007

He always told me that I needed to get an education because a degree is very important, and I agreed. So, I started Rockland Community College. I decided that I was ready, and I wanted a career—one that I would be able to support myself if needed. Brian told me that if I did well, he would help me pay back my student loans. When he left last summer, there was an e-mail that he sent me, and he stated something about how I should consider quitting school because it was going to be more debt for me to pay back because the storm was coming soon. It turned out that I currently have a 4.0 GPA and I am a member of the Phi Theta Kappa Honor Society.

Even though I have a great GPA, Brian said to me that there was a difference between being book smart and having common sense. It didn't matter what kind of GPA I had because to him, I was still stupid. Now that I am living in New Jersey, I am not currently enrolled in a school. I did get accepted into Essex County College; however, I learned at the beginning of December that they do not take the student loans that I have. The only take credit-based loans which would not be good given my current credit score is 500 (bankruptcy) or a repayment plan which I also cannot do because I bring home $395/week and I have a car payment, car insurance (doubled in New Jersey), storage bill, cell phone, food, medical debt, etc. I applied for financial aid but was turned down because $395/week is still considered too much money to receive help.

December 2007

We went across the street to a Christmas party at our neighbor's house. At this point, I had become so accustomed to being insulted and ridiculed. The next day, I had been talking to my neighbor Mary Beth and she started talking about the party. She said that everyone believes I am suffering from some form of abuse. Not only was he putting me down in front of them, but he was going on and on about how happy he was that he no longer allowed the dogs upstairs because he knew I wanted to be anywhere they were and now he doesn't have to see me at night because I was with them, in the basement. Everyone there thought it was awful, but me, I laughed it off. Did I really know what he was doing or was I so broken that I thought it was all my fault? I remember feeling anger at the accusation from my neighbor. I did what I did best—make excuses for him, for everything he said or did.

*****

One night I took the 5:42 p.m. train back home (train departed from Hoboken and our stop was in Tuxedo, New York). Brian was not on the train. He called me on my cell phone and told me that he would be on the next train (6:27 p.m.). Since he had the keys to the car, he told me to wait across the street for him in the little deli. I did, and while I was there, I decided to put the labels and stamps on the Christmas cards that I wanted to send out. When the train came in, he pulled up and I got into the car with him. He pulled away so fast and I did not realize that the door was not fully shut. As he made the left at the light, my door opened and the box of Christmas cards that were on my lap started to fall out. I told him to please stop the car so I can pick them up. After all, I had just spent money on them, and I did not have the money to go out and buy more. I had taken a picture of my bulldog Bubba and made up Christmas cards at CVS—so it was not cheap. I got out of the car and tried chasing the cards down. Meanwhile he stayed in the car and yelled at me and started calling me all kinds of names. When I got back in the car, he lectured me the whole way home.

When we got home, the lecture started, and we had another argument. Now by the time he was done with his lecture, it was 9:00 p.m. and I still had to take care of the dogs, feed all the animals, take my shower, and try and be in bed by 10:00 p.m.

Since I worked in New York City, I had to get up every day at 5:00 a.m. to make the 6:19 a.m. train out of Tuxedo, New York. That was not going to happen. Brian told me that I had to steam clean the basement which was 1,700 square feet. I asked him if I could do it another night since I was tired and had to get up early, but the answer was "no" and if I did not do it, he would get rid of three dogs—the ones he hated the most, Toby, Lily, and Jack. So, I went downstairs and did the steam cleaning. I was done about 12:30 a.m. When I came upstairs, we started to have another argument and he threw his Gatorade against the wall and it splashed all over the place. Since I caused him to throw his Gatorade, I was ordered to go out and buy him another one. So, I got in the car and drove to the Exxon station down the road and got him a new one. When I got home, he was in bed sleeping and I took my shower and finally went to bed at 2:00 a.m. and had to get up at 5:00 a.m. I did not sleep right away though. I was upset and nervous and knew what tomorrow would bring—the silent treatment and the cold shoulder.

March 20, 2008

I was at work when I received a call from the mortgage company regarding the papers that we submitted on February 14 for a loan modification. I called Brian and did a conference call with the mortgage representative because he needed to go over our financials with us. Brian advised the representative that he was currently out of work and that his termination date from his previous job was February 16, 2008. When the representative heard this, we were denied a loan modification and advised that our house was being put in foreclosure. I was devastated. I started to cry and decided to leave work early for the day.

When I got home, I was crying and scared, and Brian started yelling at me and did not want to hear me cry because according to him, I am the reason that we lost the house. He told me that he was going to start packing and that I should as well. I asked him where we were going to live and he said, "Well I am going to get my own place—so you have to figure out where you are going to go with the animals." I asked him if he was leaving me and he said he might. He told me that he might take me with him, but there were no promises and that he and only he will make that decision. I felt so alone and even more scared than ever. Instead of supporting each other, he was threatening me and putting more fear into me along with guilt—telling me that this was my entire fault and to "suck it up."

Saturday, June 2008

This was the last day that I had seen Brian's parents. We went into Goshen that day and picked up some chocolate-covered strawberries, and then he drove us to his parents' boat in Newburgh, New York. We hung out with them for a while on the boat, and then we all went out to dinner. Everything seemed to be going well until the foreclosure was brought up. I started saying something to his parents about how the mortgage company has been contacting me every day to see if we qualify for a new loan modification since Brian started working again. Brian flipped out and started to yell at me in front of his parents and then we left the restaurant and headed home. Throughout the whole car ride home, he yelled at me so badly and threatened me again that he would leave me and told me that I will never be allowed to go on his parents' boat again.

May 2008

Brian lost his job on February 16, 2008, and had still been out of work. I had come home from work, and as I was walking into the foyer, I looked upstairs and saw Brian's closet door in the hallway and busted furniture lying all over the floor. I ran upstairs and asked him what happened and if he was OK. He said, "Go away—you did this to me. You caused all of this. You have made me lose all my patience. This is your fault." I had no idea what he was referring to. I had been at work all day and didn't even speak to him on the phone that day. He had busted a piece of furniture from his office and ripped his closed door off the wall and even damaged the wall in his office (pictures attached).

Months later, I was talking with Jeanne and Andy Smith about that day and all the destruction, and I found out what he had blamed me for. Apparently, he lost a bid on eBay and he blamed me for losing that bid because I caused him to lose his focus. I wasn't even there and had nothing to do with it.

Thursday, July 3, 2008

Brian had started his new job with ING at the beginning of June. He would leave on Monday mornings for Connecticut and come home on Friday nights. I don't even know what hotel he would stay at—he never gave me the information. All I had was his cell phone to get in touch with him. Every time he came home, he would ignore me—not even acknowledge my presence. Sometimes I would be in the basement and hear him come home and wait and see if he would come to say, "Hello," or even say "I am home."

Well on this day, I was downstairs with the dogs and I hear him come home. I waited and waited, but nothing. This was starting to make me upset because I was so tired of being disrespected, ignored, and constantly getting the silent treatment. I went upstairs and he was sitting in his office on the computer already. I said to him, "Hi, Brian. How are you, Brian? How was your day, Brian. I am here." With that he blew up and started calling me foul names.

He then said, "I was going to say that we should go to the movies and dinner tonight, but since you are nasty, we are not going. I might go by myself—you don't deserve anything nice." I started crying and then the argument began. I ran up to the bunny hutch and sat with the baby bunnies and started crying. I just couldn't take this anymore.

When I came back inside, Brian was sitting in the chair in the family room watching TV. I decided to sit with him and watch the show on TV. I even remember what it was—it was a documentary about a U.S. woman who got arrested in Australia for carrying marijuana on her. I found it interesting and wanted to continue watching it. After the show was over, Brian started screaming at me and accused me of sitting there with him to spy on him and not giving him any space. He then threw the remote control into the wall which left a hole in the wall (pictures attached). Then he got more vicious, and he took the silk plant holder that was on the counter and threw it across the room and it busted all over the rug. Then he said he was leaving me. I turned to him and said, "Fine, if you want to leave, then leave, but you are not taking anything with you since I purchased everything in this house."

With that, he walked into the foyer and kicked the glass vase that was standing on the floor next to the Victorian chair. The vase shattered all over the place. I followed him upstairs and begged him to please not leave and asked him why he was doing this to me. I tried to pull him back from leaving and he took me and pushed me away and I almost fell down the stairs. I followed him outside to his car and was begging to please, please, not leave me. He then took me again and pushed me to the ground. I fell on the wood that was sitting next to the bunny hutch since the handyman had left all the wood there. The nails from the wood had gone through my pants and into my leg. I was crying so hard and started to hyperventilate. I watched him get into his car and drive away.

I called my parents and told them that Brian left me and that I felt like I was going crazy and I was scared. I also called the police and told them that I think I need mobile mental health because my husband left home after a big fight and I am feeling unstable. Brian then called me and said he saw the cops going to the house and he was coming right back. When he got there, I was hysterical. Never, ever, in my life has anyone broken me down to this point. Once the cops came, everything starts to become fuzzy. I remember telling the cops that I fell off the ladder by the bunny hutch and hurt my own knee because I did not want Brian to get even madder at me and then leave me. Also, when I currently looked at the police report from that night, I called Sergeant Mullins and told him that I was very upset by the report because I was never given a chance to tell my side of the story and what really happened because I had been taken away to the hospital at that point.

Brian falsely stated that I started verbally abusing him when he came home from work and that I was the one who damaged many items in the house. Luckily my parents were there while the cops were questioning Brian, and my dad said to Brian, "You are a liar." Sergeant Mullins said that I told him I broke the vase and that I hurt my own knee; however, being in this profession for twenty years, he said he has seen this before where the abused woman covers for her husband. He told me that he was talking to my parents and they all pretty much summed it up—once my money was gone, so was Brian. (Sergeant Mullins said he would be willing to talk to my lawyer about that night if needed.) Sergeant Mullins stated that even though I hated him that night for bringing me to the hospital, he knew he was doing the right thing by getting me out of that house and away from him.

I was taken to St. Anthony's Hospital around 11:00 p.m. and kept there until the morning in which I was transferred to Bon Secours in Port Jervis, New York. I remember screaming and crying that I wanted to go home and that I was not suicidal. I felt trapped, and all I could think about was Brian leaving me. It was one of the worst experiences in my life—a time in my life that I pray I can completely forget one day.

The next morning, I was taken to Bon Secours and told that I had to stay there for seventy-two hours. I was screaming and crying and wanted to get out of there. All I could think about was Brian leaving me since he had threatened me repeatedly over the years. I called him several times during my stay there from a payphone, and he refused to pick up the phone. He didn't even call me to see how I was doing. My mother had called him and told him that I needed clothes and my birth control pills because it was a Catholic hospital and they would not give me the pills—I had to have my own pills taken to me. On Sunday, July 6, I found out that my husband came very late and dropped off some clothes for me and all my medications. He didn't even bother to come during visiting hours to check up on me. I was devastated, lonely, scared, and very depressed.

I was released on Monday, July 7. My mother and father and Aunt Vicki were with me. They took me back to the house, and I faced my worst nightmare—Brian moved out. I broke down. He had taken 90 percent of his belongings and moved into his parent's house in Pomona, New York. I called him and wanted to know why, and he said it was all my fault and I made him leave the home and he was never coming back and that we were done.

I didn't know what I was going to do with anything. First, the house was in foreclosure status, and I didn't know what to do. If I left, I would forfeit, and the one thing that mortgage companies hate is when people just abandon the house. It leaves the house open to theft and damage. I felt I still had a responsibility there. Plus, my parents were not ready for me to move in yet. They were struggling with their own bills and were behind on their mortgage because my father's business had been slow.

Second, I had a stack of bills that needed to be paid and I had no money. When Brian lost his job in February 2008, we only had my income plus his $405/week from unemployment. In the meantime, we fell behind on the house bills. He started his job in June 2008. I, myself, lost my job on May 20, 2008, and started collecting $405/week from unemployment as well. I found my current job on July 1, 2008. I started a temporary job at Toys R Us in Wayne, New Jersey. My hourly rate was $22/hour at forty hours/week. The money still was not enough.

Since I was on a temporary status, I was offered no benefits or paid time off. If I missed a day of work, there was no pay. I struggled every day. Brian did not offer to help with bills at all. The only thing he told me to do was take his VA check that came in once a month ($376) and deposit it into the joint account and then move it into my account and pay the car insurance with that which was $220/month. He then told me to take the rest and keep it for myself. That was all he gave me. The electric bill itself was just about $500/month. To say the least, I was scared, and Brian wanted nothing to do with the house or the bills. I had some hope that our marriage would work out and I even tried to still save the house and work out a new loan modification with the mortgage company.

September 2008

I came home from work one day and started opening the mail. I opened a bank statement that I thought was for our joint account at Bank of America. I opened the statement and suddenly realized that it was not for the joint account, but for Brian's personal account. As I looked at it, I started to cry. All the time I had been struggling to pay bills, he had been going out having a good time spending money. I noticed some charges from a night in August that he went to bars, restaurants, and Lace—a gentlemen's club—and spent quite a bit of money. I even called the club and found out the price of a lap dance because I saw two separate charges for $95. I called him and started to cry to him. I felt too hurt. He said that he was stressed out and needed to release stress. I was stressed too—after all, he had walked out on me and left me in a foreclosed home with all the bills, bills that he was not intending to contribute to.

October 31, 2008–November 2008

I got paperwork from the mortgage company regarding a new loan modification. I was hoping to surprise Brian, and I even had hope that this would bring him home and me and him back together. I didn't tell him that I had been working on this because I wanted it to be a surprise. I had given our current financials—his salary from his new job, my salary, and our monthly operating expenses. They were going to give us a three months' trial period, and if we paid on time, the payments would either stay the same or go down after three months. They took our current mortgage rate of $5,164/month—not escrowed to $4,800/month which would include taxes and insurance.

I talked to our friend Andy and asked if he would present this to Brian since Brian never listens to anything that I have to say and always puts down any decisions that I make. Andy finally did talk to him, but Brian was adamant and insisted that he would not go along with it and that he was never going to come back home and that we were getting divorced. I called Brian to talk to him about this, and he screamed at me and started putting me down once again. I asked him to please not yell as much because I was sick all day with a migraine and he knew what happened to me when I had gotten those. He didn't care and continued to scream at me.

End of November–December 2008

I started making calls to realtors inquiring about houses to rent. I didn't have the income to support a place to rent, but I wanted to get some idea of what was out there. I got in touch with Jodi of Prudential located in Suffern, New York. I explained my current situation, and she asked me if we had an attorney for the foreclosure. She suggested that I call an attorney that they work with. His name is Harry Redding of Ryan and Redding in Suffern, New York. I called him and he asked me to call his associate Mark Sanchez. I called him and discussed our situation. He suggested that we meet up on that Saturday morning at Café Ala Mode in Warwick and go over everything. When we met, I told him that there was no way I could afford the retainer fee, and he suggested making monthly payments of $500, but I still was not able to afford that. I talked to him again that week, and he said that I really needed to get Brian involved because if the house goes into full foreclosure, they will garnish both of our wages for the rest of our life. I asked him to call Brian and discuss this with him because I feared Brian and did not want to deal with the tears or the name-calling or the screaming. He called Brian and talked to him and told me that Brian agreed to getting involved in this and that we were going to meet at their offices on Saturday, December 13.

The night before our meeting, I had called Brian and he asked me if I would bring Russell and Bubba with me because he had not seen them in a long time and wanted to see them (Russell and Bubba were two of his favorite dogs). I said something to him, and he lashed back at me saying, "We are never going to get back together—get that through that thick skull of yours." I started crying and he hung up on me which was typical of him.

Throughout our whole marriage, he would always hang up the phone on me, and that was one thing I could not stand. I considered it rude. I called him back, and he yelled at me even more and told me that now he was not going to go to the meeting with Marty and he hung up again and shut off his phone.

The next day, I left the house and called Marty from the road and told him that Brian and I had an argument the night before and I was not sure if he was going to show up for our meeting. When I arrived at the office, Brian arrived a few minutes later. We met with Marty and Brian, and I signed the retainer agreement. Marty said to me that I now have a year or more left in the house—which was good news to me because I did not have anywhere to go at the present time. When we left the meeting, Brian and I took Bubba and Russell to the dog park and that is when Brian took out some Christmas gifts for me and then for the dogs. I was so happy and really thought there was a chance for us. I asked him to please reconsider coming back, but he said no and that he just got me the gifts so that I could have a nice Christmas. I asked him if he was doing anything for Christmas eve and if not to please consider doing something with me because I was lonely. When I got home, he texted me and said Christmas eve was good for him if I was still up to it.

Saturday, October 3, 2009

My husband called me up and confessed to me that he met Alana K. Jones on March 10, 2009, from an escort service ad listed on Craig's List where he paid her $800 for sex.

After that night, they started dating, and around May, they became exclusive and she moved in with him when he purchased his townhouse in White Plains on September 1, 2009.

A few days prior to October 3, they had broken up and on Saturday, October 3, while Brian was out all day, Alana along with her sister Rupinder moved her stuff out of his townhouse, but in the process, Alana stole many items. He told me that he was going to the White Plains police department to file a report (case #105090428). Also, he was nervous because he said that she told him that she could have him "taken out." He said that she had many connections such as drug pushers and pimps and he was nervous for his life and for his possessions. He even had the locks changed on his apartment or at least he told me he was doing that. He also told me that he was going to try and be around people as much as he could so that he would always have an alibi—just in case she lied to the police and told them that he tried contacting her or went near her. He told me that in the event I called or text him and he does not respond to please call his parents immediately and tell them because it could mean that something happened to him. He told me he was that scared and that I should be careful as well because she was crazy and her connections were dangerous.

Then he said to me, "Do you know your buddy Greg Driscoll? Well that was Alana and has been all along."

The "Greg Driscoll" Story

I n June 16, 2009, after numerous friend requests on Facebook, I finally accepted a "Greg Driscoll" friend request. In June 16, 2009–October 3, 2009, "Robert Driscoll" and I had been e-mailing each other and using the Facebook and America Online chat features to talk with each other.

He said Alana got her friend Harry Robinson involved, and they were both doing the e-mails and chatting. It started out as her Googling me to try and get "dirt" on me and spy on me. She had been paranoid about Brian cheating on her with me. I also come to find out that the woman that called me as Greg Driscoll's sister "Kim" was her. Brian stated that he knew about Alana engaging in this since June and did not tell me sooner because he was worried about jeopardizing his relationship with her. He also stated that Alana made all these e-mails from her computer and iPhone that he had purchased for her. To say the least, I was devastated and shocked.

On Friday, August 21, at approximately 11:30 p.m., I received a call from a private number. I answered and the woman on the other end said it was "Kim," Greg's sister from Westchester. She said that Greg had called her husband, a White Plains cop, and asked him to please have Kim call me and check up on me because Greg was worried about me being all alone up there. We had a conversation 'til 1:30 a.m. When we hung up, she said she would call me tomorrow to check up on me, but she never did call. I placed two phone calls to her over the week to thank her for talking to me, but she never returned my phone calls, and when I called her number, there was no external message saying her name. It just said the number and to leave a message.

During those four months, I did get a little suspicious because he only e-mailed me and chatted with me but never called me, and he supposedly left for London on August 14, spent a week there, and flew out to Ireland that following weekend and then he had to go to Stockholm for work on an investment and did not know when he would be returning, but he did tell me that once he returned, we would get together and that I was not going to be alone for the holidays or my birthday because he was going to take me to be with his family.

Greg told me that he lived in West New York, New Jersey, and that his company, HSBC, paid for his living arrangements and that he moves around a lot. He said that when he gets back from Stockholm, the company will be moving him again—either to a place in New York or New Jersey. Greg constantly asked me for photographs of myself claiming that he thought I was beautiful and loved looking at my photographs. He also asked a lot of personal questions about me and Brian, my divorce, etc.

He asked for my resume at one point, telling me that he would forward it to his contacts and help me find a job. Greg also had my phone numbers, home address, and work address. I, being in a vulnerable state, believed every word. It felt so good to feel needed, wanted, and complimented since I experienced much verbal and mental abuse in my marriage. I have been alone since the weekend of July 4, 2008, when my husband left home. I have been through so much financially and emotionally and for once, I was feeling happy. There were times that I felt suspicious, but the more and more he e-mailed me with sincere e-mails, I would put those feelings aside. One thing did bother me for sure is that all his e-mails were from an e-mail address called keepinguloved@aol.com (suspicious e-mail address) and the fact that he chatted with me at odd times—when it would have been 4:00 a.m. in Stockholm. I was stupid and naïve.

*****

47

That night when he told me all of this, I was hysterically crying. I felt violated and deceived and could not believe that my husband allowed her to do this to me. I do not understand why they could not just leave me alone. It was a sick practical joke and it was hurtful. I poured my heart out to someone who did not exist. Brian called me several times that night—one time being 2:00 a.m.—saying that he was at a bar and that I should come to White Plains and hang out with him one weekend and that he would help me find someone if I helped him find someone too. I could not believe he was acting like this.

Sunday, October 4, 2009

S till in shock over everything, I called his parents because one thing concerned me very much—Brian experimenting with cocaine. He told me that Alana was a heavy drug user and that one night he tried cocaine with her because he was worried about her and wanted to be in the same state of mind as her. This really, really, concerned me because my husband in his past never ever did drugs before—he was straight. I felt that his parents should know because he might need help. To me, cocaine is very serious and, from what I have read, very addicting and people lose everything—jobs, friends, family, money, etc.

His mother answered the phone and I told her. When I told her, I was also crying—still trying to grasp everything I learned from the night before. His mother told me that she was never happy about this relationship with her and that they were going to change the locks on their house as well. They never trusted her, and now they were worried about their son because of her connections. To them, she was dangerous. I spoke with his dad as well who said they were going to have a discussion with him. After I hung up with them, Brian called me later and yelled at me for calling them and accused me of yelling at them. I told him that I thought they should know because that is a dangerous drug and I was worried about him. I told him that I was not going to feel bad about caring for someone else's welfare. He was still my husband and I was worried.

Monday, October 5, 2009

B rian called me and told me he was served by the police with
an Order of Protection (OP) that she placed against him. He
gave me the file and docket number so that I could get a copy
of it (which I did not realize 'til recently that you cannot obtain a
copy of them) and that when I file the harassment charges against
her, I should give the cops this information. She stated in the Order
of Protection that she would try and leave the apartment and he
would take her keys away so she could not leave and then force her
to have sex, he harassed her, and he stalked her. He told me that his
court date was Friday, December 4, and asked me if I could come
with him to court to defend him. He even put me in contact with the
attorney that he was supposed to be retaining for this matter.

Tuesday, October 6, 2009

Since I moved back to West Orange to live with my parents on October 3, I went to the West Orange Police Department and filed a report with Officer Cullen against Alana Jones for harassment and impersonation. Two days later, my report was ready, and I took the report to the court clerk and filled out the appropriate forms and was told that she was going to receive a summons to come to court. The court date was scheduled for Tuesday, October 20.

When I told Brian that she was going to be summoned, he was so excited and said, "I just want to hug you right now. Oh, this is great—I wish I could see her face. I hope she goes to jail for this. She escaped the law so many times before and now she deserves to get locked up." Also, before I got to the police station, Brian asked me if I could call his parents and apologize for freaking out on them the other day. Because I still cared about him, I told him yes and called them and spoke with his dad. We had a good conversation, and he told me that he told Brian to just drop everything because this girl is capable of much and he fears for his son and was even afraid for me because she could come after me.

Since I had just moved back to West Orange and the majority of all the e-mails had been done in Warwick, I was told that I should also go to the Warwick Police Department and file charges there as well. I called them and had a lengthy conversation with Bill. I asked him if my husband would get into trouble for paying an escort for sex because I really did not want to get him into trouble and my husband was getting nervous that he would get a criminal record for that. He said no and that it would be best if we both come together to speak with a detective.

Saturday, October 10, 2009

I met Brian at the Warwick Police Department to file charges against Alana. We met with Detective Neiman. He took a full report from both of us. Brian made a full confession (one part listed on police report) that he had paid her for sex and then carried on a relationship with her. He also told Detective Neiman about her drug use, and Detective Neiman had asked him if he knew where she had gotten her drugs from. Brian carried a manila folder with him filled with her sex ads from Craig's List. Detective Neiman told him that he did not need to see them since I was the one filing the harassment charges. Brian made sure that Detective Neiman knew Alana was a threat because of her connections between drug pushers and pimps. I sat there and cried my eyes out. No woman likes to hear about her husband's fling with another woman—especially a paid prostitute.

Sunday, October 11, 2009

Brian's parents were coming over his townhouse for dinner. Brian had invited me to come as well, but I did not want to go because I did not feel comfortable about walking into a home that my husband shared with another woman and I do not drive over bridges and in order to get to his townhouse, I would have to drive over the bridge and there was no way that I was able to do that. He was trying to be around people as much so that if Alana tried to lie and say that he violated the Order of Protection, he would always have an alibi.

Monday, October 12, 2009

Brian called me just to talk. He told me how he thought this experience was bringing us closer together. He also said, "I should not be telling you this, but I told my parents yesterday that there might even be a chance of us getting back together one day."

Thursday, October 15, 2009

I called Brian in the morning, but there was no answer. I then sent him a text message, but still no response. I got very nervous because that was not like him. He had said to me that if I call him or text him and do not get a response, call his parents and let them know because that could mean something happened to him. He was worried about Alana having one of her connections come after him or even having someone slash his tires or break his windows on his truck.

I called his dad and told him that I was not getting a response from Brian and that I was worried. He thanked me and said he would try and get in touch with him and then call me back. After one hour and no response from Brian or his dad, I called his dad again. His dad said that he did get in touch with him at work, but he had been charging his phone which is why he was not responding. Since I do not know where Brian works or do not even have his work number, his dad was my only contact.

Brian texted me and said that we needed to talk about the harassment charges against Alana. I had a funny feeling it was going to be something about dropping them. Well, I called him immediately and asked him what is going on. He told me that Alana had called him the night before and told him that if I pursue the harassment charges, she will pursue the Order of Protection against him. He begged me to drop them because if she pursues the OP, then he could possibly get criminal charges against him and then he would lose his job and not be able to pay the foreclosure attorney and the taxes or even give me spousal support one day. He asked me to please do this for him.

I blew up. I could not believe what I was hearing. After what she had put me through and now I was supposed to drop everything. I told him that I needed to call him from my cell phone outside because I did not want to fight in the office. I went outside and called him and had a huge argument with him. I told him that if I do this for him, then he needed to promise me that he would never speak to her again or ever get back to her. I asked him where his loyalty was—to the woman he said his vows to or an escort who takes money for sex. He told me that he would not get back with her but that I also did not have the right to tell him what to do.

After that day, I completely lost my temper. After all that I had been through between his abuse, his abandonment, the food pantries, social services, his girlfriend's deception (and his), and so much more, I lost it. Anger, bitterness, hate, and depression hit an all-time high. From that point, I was guilty of writing him e-mails or texts with nasty jabs because I was so hurt, more than anyone will ever know and I was angry, I felt betrayed. I could not help but call his girlfriend an escort because to me, that is all she is—a woman who takes money for sex and then lives off other men's money and has no care if they are married or not. She had deceived me, taken money from him, and accepted gifts from him all while I was suffering and going to food pantries and social services. Now my husband had loyalty to her and not me—his wife. I was there for him when he was running from her and even forgave him and now he was protecting her. I became so very depressed—more than I had ever felt before.

Monday, December 7, 2009

About a week before December 7 in one of the e-mails between me, Brian, and the mediator, Marty Wolk, he had asked me to stop calling her an escort. Once I heard that, I had a feeling that he was back with her—especially because he had suddenly cut off all communication with me starting in early November. (Honestly, that hurt. Believe it or not, but I did love my husband; no matter what he did to me, I thought I was going to change him and make him love me and make our marriage perfect—like the kind of woman he wanted, perfect.) I sent him a separate e-mail and asked him if he was back with her because I wanted to hear it from him and not someone else. He told me that after being nasty to him, he was not going to answer me. I cried and swore that I would never speak with him again. I hated being deceived and having my heart broken over and over.

On Monday, December 7, my phone rang, and I saw that it was Brian calling me. I refused to pick up the phone and just let it go to voice mail. I checked for a message but saw that he did not leave one. He then called over and over but would not leave a message—just kept calling. I texted him and told him to stop calling me and go and talk to his "escort." He kept calling. I then picked up and told him to never call me again. He then told me that he and Alana had reconciled, and they were now living together (again) and they wanted a future together and that I should just move on with my life. I started crying and screaming and then he put Alana on the phone with me who also started yelling at me (as if I was not hurt enough and now I was having the other woman yell at me and my husband was allow-ing it). She had called me a "fat pig" and said things like she is going to have his baby someday and that she is the one who is fucking my husband now.

I eventually hung up on him, but when my mom came home and saw me crying and hyperventilating, she called him and told him off. She also said that he was slurring his words. When I talked to him, he sounded like he was drunk or high. After my mom hung up with him, he kept calling. Finally, I called the West Orange cops and they sent an officer to the house. Brian called with the officer at my house and the cop told me to pick up and tell him that he was there and that I was filing harassment charges. Brian then said, "Great," and I hung up on him.

I cannot begin to tell you the pain that I felt in my heart.

Thursday, December 10, 2009

I was home doing my banking online when I noticed that the joint account was missing. I immediately called Wachovia, and they told me that the account was closed. I asked them who had closed it, and they were not able to see who did it. The account had no money in it. We only had the account open for spousal support payments (which I never received). I then had a very worried feeling hit me. Brian had my Social Security number from the times that we did out taxes together. I do not trust him or her at all. He gave me her Social Security number so easily (I did not even ask for it)—so what is to say that he has not given her mine. When I asked him how he got her Social Security number, he had told me that he had it because he made her car payments for her and paid off her debt.

I then proceeded to ask the customer service representative if anyone had called regarding my account. She said that I had called just yesterday—which is funny since I had not called at all! I immediately called the West Orange Police Department, and they had an officer come by to take a report. If it had not been me, then my only suspicion was her. They have my Social Security number and all my personal information. Luckily Wachovia established a four-digit pin for me so that whenever someone calls regarding my account, they have to say or punch in that pin in order to access my account.

I called Brian and left him a message telling him that his girlfriend possibly broke into my account and that I was filing charges. He called me back and told me that I was lying because she would never do that. I had another huge argument with him. Once again, he put his girlfriend on the phone to say more hurtful things to me.

In my opinion, she has no right to get involved in my conversations with my husband. Brian called me later and left me a message saying that he knows I am hurt and that we are both out of control and to please call him. I called him back and he told me that he was alone so that we could talk. He also asked me to unblock his cell phone. On December 7, I had called Verizon and blocked his cell phone to mine, but what I did not know is that he had a landline that he started calling me from.

I called him back and told him that he had really hurt me—more than he knows.

Friday, December 11, 2009

My dad called me at work to tell me that I received a certified letter from NYS Division of Taxation. I had a feeling that it had something to do with the money that Brian owes for the 2007 taxes. I called him on his cell phone, but no answer, so I left a message. I then sent him a text message, but still nothing. I then called his house number and Alana answered. I asked if he was there and she said he was at work and I told her to tell him that "his wife called and that we got a certified letter." When I got home, I noticed that he tried calling my cell phone and I missed his call. I then called him back on his home number and once again, Alana picked up. She said, "Honey, it's for you." When I heard that, I lost it. I asked him why she felt she had to answer the phone when she clearly saw my number on the caller ID and why she must call him "honey" in front of me. I felt so hurt. We are not even divorced or legally separated and here he is living with another woman and going on with his life like I never existed.

He yelled at me and then hung up on me. I called him back because I needed to know what is going on with the taxes since my name is also on there. When I called back, she answered and then yelled at me and hung up. I then called again, and she said that she was not going to put him on the phone 'til I showed her respect because "she lives there now and she is a part of his life now." I was so mad. She was getting in the middle of a situation between husband and wife and this issue has to do with our taxes—not hers. I must have called at least five times. Finally, I gave in and tried talking to her. I was hysterically crying to her at this point. I found myself saying, "I love my husband and I want him back."

I had to sit there and listen to her and then listen to both joking around with each other. I was completely numb from the Xanax I had just taken to help with the hyperventilating and the anxiety. She even had the nerve to say to me that I will not get any spousal support from my husband because I do not show him respect. After a while of listening to her, I told her that I had to get off the phone because I was getting stomach pains from my ulcer. She must have texted me about six times from the time that I hung up with her 'til the next day (see text messages). I got so disgusted that I called Verizon and blocked both her cell phone and his home phone from my cell phone. I wanted nothing to do with either of them. The pain that I felt was so unbearable.

On another note, I did not even have the chance to discuss the tax situation with Brian. She took over the conversation, and I was at the point where I felt so sick and was in a lot of pain.

Tuesday, December 22, 2009

It started out with Brian sending an e-mail to Marty Wolk, the mediator, regarding payment and advising him as to when he should start doing the changes to the separation agreement.

What had made me even more depressed now is how he would not support me and let our house go into foreclosure; however, he is now living in a $2,500/month townhouse and living with his girlfriend of ten months who does not work and has been supporting her all along. He told me that when they decided to become exclusive, he asked her to stop hooking and working as a stripper.

He has told me that he is the best thing in my life and that if he ever leaves me, he will find someone better and that I will find a fat slob who doesn't work or care about himself because that is all that I am worth. Brian also told me that I am not a supermodel and not worth the grief that I give him.

Every time there was an argument, I feared the next day and the day after that. On top of the argument being bad between the name-calling, threats, lectures, and violent outbursts, there were the silent treatments and dirty looks that lasted for days after the fight. There were never any apologies from him, and when I apologized to him (because I really wanted the argument to end), he would not accept it, stating that it is always the same thing and that I am always the cause of the arguments. I remember waking up many times the day after an argument and I was scared, really scared because I did not know what the day had in store for me.

Throughout our marriage, I felt as if I was walking on eggshells. I did not know what the day or night would bring. Would he be in a bad mood? If an argument happened the night before, would he continue ignoring me and if so, how many more days would it last?

What else will I do that will make him mad? How can I please him today? What would set him off today?

I remember when we met with the priest that married us, he said to us, "Never go to bed mad at each other." I tried to live by that rule, but that was very hard with Brian. He went to bed mad and woke up the next day mad. It was a horrible feeling and even worse when the sun came up because I knew it would all start again.

Brian was always right, and I was always wrong.

If I mentioned my dreams or goals for the future, he would shoot them down and tell me that I could not do it (below are just some examples).

I wanted to be a mother someday. He told me that I should not be allowed to have children and that I would be a horrible mother. He told me that he would *never* have children with me.

I wanted to be a teacher (pre-K–six). That was not good enough because teachers do not make a lot of money, and there was no way he was going to support me. I needed to contribute more money to the marriage.

I wanted to get my real estate license someday, but he told me that I did not have the personality for it, and I would be no good.

He has threatened me repeatedly (just some examples):

- You better change and do a 360 or I will go to an attorney.
- I will dictate the money in this house, or I will go to an attorney.
- If you don't become a real wife, I will go to an attorney.
- Since you ruined my day, you better do the chores that I give you or I will go to an attorney.
- I am giving you two weeks to change (December 2006) or I will go to an attorney.

He has constantly punished me and given me ultimatums.

He has told me that I am the reason for his violence, temper, anger, unhappiness, financial problems, misery, and depression.

He has told me that I am the reason for him not having patience anymore, for the loss of his concentration, the reason that the neighbors never bothered with us, and the reason that he could not finish his dream bike.

He had told me repeatedly that I was the worst part of his day.

He would lose a bid on eBay and he would blame me.

He would lose a job and blame everyone but himself. It was always his boss who was the horrible person. He has repeatedly stated that he is the only one with common sense, the only smart one, and the only competent one. He said, "Everyone should be like me."

He even stated in his Order of Protection against me that I have caused him to lose jobs. In May 2004, he started working for ESP (I believe that was the name of the company). His boss' name was Adam who he had complained about and once again, it was his boss being unreasonable and not him. In June 2004, we had found the house in Warwick, New York, and before the closing that took place on August 31, 2004, there was a lot of communication going on between the realtor, real estate attorney, mortgage company, inspector, insurance agents, etc. Since Brian wanted to make all the decisions and be in the loop, I could send him e-mails or copy him on those e-mails or we would do conference calls. The day before we closed on the house, he got called into the office. He later called me and told me that they had let him go and he stated that it was my entire fault because of the constant e-mails and phone calls. At the time I believe it and felt so guilty, but as the years went on and he was constantly losing jobs, I often wondered if that was the real reason. It was always them and not him.

He would treat me and scold me like a child. There were many times I was sitting in the corner of the kitchen (between the hallway to the foyer and the dining room) and I was being lectured by him. I was not allowed to answer the phone, get a drink, go to the bathroom, look the other way, speak up, and defend myself. I was not allowed to move at all while he was lecturing me. It was my fault that he had to lecture me, and now I had to listen to him. He would talk for an hour—sometimes more—and then when he was done, and I was allowed to get up and do my own thing. Sometimes after the lecture, I was given chores to do by him. He told me that I made him lecture me like a child and in turn, I caused him to waste his time and therefore, I had to make the time up to him. That meant that I had to do chores for him such as cleaning his car or run out and get him his power drinks (those are just a few examples).

Decisions—even the smallest of ones—were made by him. He told me that every decision I made was wrong and always got us into trouble. I was not trusted making any decisions. I remember back in May 2007, my attorney Barry Weinstein had sent me the summons and complaint to my former employer, The Bond Companies. When he saw how much money Barry was seeking, he told me that if I win, he would control all the money—not me even though this was my disability case. In fact, we went to dinner that night to the Crystal Inn in Amity, New York. While we were at dinner, he started telling me some of the things he would do with the money—including finishing his bike and making his dream come true. He even stated that he wanted to help Alex out (Alex was his friend from Motorcycle World). I objected and said no, but I was quickly shut down. He told me that he will do what he wants, and if I don't like it, he will go to an attorney.

Through it all, I stayed with him because I did love him. He swept me off my feet with his charm and his affection and drastically changed once we moved in together. My family and friends did not like him from the minute they met him, and they saw right through him—everyone but me. I also stayed because I was afraid of finances, the house, and losing my animals because I had so many and was afraid of us having nowhere to go together. Plus, I did not believe in divorce and really thought he was going to change and that I was going to be the one to make him change. My parents were separated many years ago, but together they worked on their marriage and have been married since 1969. Therefore, I had the belief that couples should work on their marriage because marriage is sacred and something that should be valued.

Though the above story is sad and tragic, that chapter is over with. My new journey just began. On October 14, I performed in my first play *Not Just October* and did it again on December 16 and will be performing again in May—more to come. He could not break me. My new journey has come.

*****

I loved my husband and I wanted to make things work. I set so set on being the one who could change him. What I didn't realize back than is that I don't have the power to change anyone who doesn't want to change. I have regrets. I have days where my heart feels such sadness of what could have been had he not abused me. I ignored the still small voice that night in April 2003. Insecurity led me into the arms of someone who had only one intention, to destroy me. The good news is that the didn't. The enemy came in like a flood, but God was there protecting me through it all. He loved me and guided me. My journey has been rough and painful, but I believe that there was a purpose in the pain. On October 14th, I performed in my first stage play called "Not Just October".

"Not Just October" is an inspirational play that was created to shed light on the realities of Domestic Violence. We, the participants in the play, are all survivors and our stories are real. I had been so lost and broken for such a long time that I doubted my ability to perform in this play. The words that had been spoken over me through all those years were constantly following me around. I lost my voice and

I lost "me". Losing a voice also meant that I was not able to speak in front 5 people let alone 215 people. But I did it. I stood on a stage in front of 215 people and shared my story. The words flowed out of my mouth and as they did, I felt a weight being lifted from my shoulders. I realized that I was no longer a prisoner to the evil that tried to destroy me. I am a survivor, I am strong, I am worth it, I am unstoppable, and I am powerful because through it all, God has been on my side, lifting me up and holding me through every storm.

My story goes on. It does not end with me falling in love or getting married again. My story ends with me, picking up the pieces of my life and putting them back together. Rebuilding friendships and my entire life. My story ends with "me" being found.

You can be found too. Never give up. Push through all the pain. No matter how dark it gets, don't stop. Keep going. Believe that you are going to make it. Scream and cry if you need to but keep moving. Trust that God will see you through it. You are not alone. You are not crazy. You are not the one that ruined the marriage. You are not worthless. You are not "washed-up". The words that they speak over you is them, looking at themselves in the mirror. You deserve to be happy. You can't change them, so don't even try. There is hep out there. I have scars that I wish would just go away; however, if my scars can help someone else, then I will keep them. I am beautifully broken.

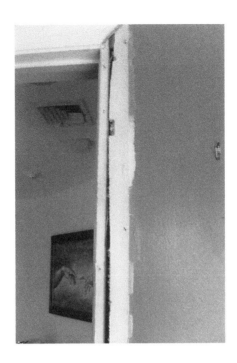

Pictures below have been documented to show his wrath when I did not listen or I was blamed for his anger, violence, temper, etc. The pictures will never leave my mind nor any victim's mind. This is real.

About the Author

Marisa was born and raised in West Orange, New Jersey. She attended West Orange High School where she graduated in June 1992. Marisa eventually went on to attend some college, but due to financial reasons and life-changing circumstances, she was not able to finish. She currently lives in the Greater New York area with her family and beloved pets. Marisa enjoys music, scrapbooking, exercising, and spending time with friends. Her love of helping others came after she found herself in an abusive marriage. Marisa vowed to take her pain and turn it around so she can help other women in similar circumstances.